THIS LAND CALLED AMERICA: **MISSISSIPPI**

CREATIVE EDUCATION

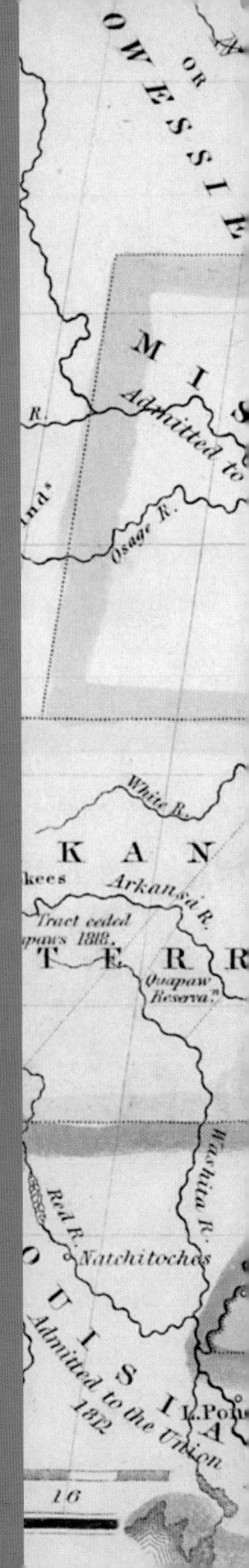

Published by Creative Education
P.O. Box 227, Mankato, Minnesota 56002
Creative Education is an imprint of The Creative Company
www.thecreativecompany.us

Book and cover design by Blue Design (www.bluedes.com)
Art direction by Rita Marshall
Printed in the United States of America

Photographs by Corbis (Tom Brakefield, Richard Cummins, Raymond
Gehman, Philip Gould, Danny Lehman, Lisa O'Connor/ZUMA, Richard
Hamilton Smith), Getty Images (Altrendo Nature, Michael Busselle,
Currier and Ives, T. C. Lindsay, Michael Ochs Archives, MPI, Carl
Mydans//Time Life Pictures, David Savill/Topical Press Agency, Stock
Montage, Mario Tama, Medford Taylor/National Geographic, Time Life
Pictures/Timepix/Time Life Pictures, Kevin Winter)

Library of Congress Cataloging-in-Publication Data
Shofner, Shawndra.
Mississippi / by Shawndra Shofner.
p. cm. — (This land called America)
Includes bibliographical references and index.
ISBN 978-1-58341-649-5
1. Mississippi—Juvenile literature. I. Title. II. Series.
F341.3.S557 2008
976.2—dc22   2007019626

First Edition
9 8 7 6 5 4 3 2 1

This Land Called America

MISSISSIPPI

Shawndra Shofner

Mississippi

SHAWNDRA SHOFNER

EACH JUNE, ONE OF MISSISSIPPI'S MOST
IMPORTANT INDUSTRIES, SHRIMPING, STARTS ITS
SEASON WITH A TRADITIONAL CEREMONY CALLED
THE BLESSING OF THE FLEET. SINCE 1929, SILENT
CROWDS HAVE GATHERED ALONG THE HARBOR OF
BILOXI BAY TO WATCH A SOLEMN WATER PARADE.
PEOPLE BOW THEIR HEADS AS FISHERMEN DROP AN
EVERGREEN WREATH INTO THE WATER IN MEMORY
OF THOSE WHO HAVE BEEN LOST AT SEA. AS
MORE THAN 30 DECORATED SHRIMP BOATS FLOAT
PAST THE "BLESSING BOAT," A CATHOLIC PRIEST
SPRINKLES HOLY WATER ON THEM AND PRAYS FOR
A SAFE AND SUCCESSFUL SEASON. SHRIMPING IS
SERIOUS BUSINESS IN MISSISSIPPI.

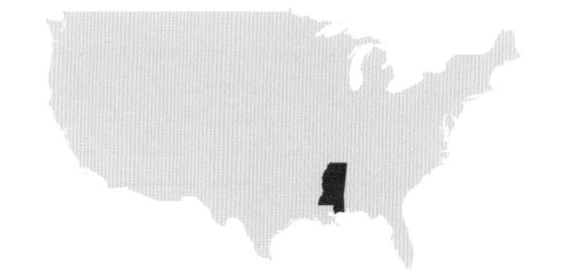

YEAR

1540 Spanish explorer Hernando de Soto travels through Mississippi looking for gold.

EVENT

French Frontier

THREE MAJOR AMERICAN INDIAN NATIONS LIVED, HUNTED, AND FARMED IN THE LANDS THAT WOULD BECOME THE STATE OF MISSISSIPPI. THESE TRIBES INCLUDED THE CHICKASAW, CHOCTAW, AND NATCHEZ. THE CHICKASAW LIVED IN THE NORTH, THE CHOCTAW IN THE CENTRAL AREAS, AND THE NATCHEZ IN THE SOUTHWEST.

Pierre Le Moyne was a local hero for fighting the English where he grew up near Montreal, Canada.

In 1540, Spanish explorer Hernando de Soto crossed what would become the state of Mississippi and discovered the river of the same name. More than 100 years later, in 1682, French explorer René-Robert de La Salle traveled from Canada to the Gulf of Mexico. He claimed Mississippi for France, along with all land west of the Mississippi River to the Rocky Mountains and north from the Gulf of Mexico to Canada. He named the vast territory Louisiana after France's King Louis XIV.

King Louis XIV sent two French brothers to govern Louisiana. In 1699, Pierre Le Moyne founded Fort Maurepas at what is now Ocean Springs, Mississippi. It was named the territorial capital. Pierre's brother Jean-Baptiste established Fort Rosalie at Natchez. That outpost quickly became populated with

The Choctaw Indian tribe of Mississippi played a ball game that involved tall goalposts.

YEAR
1682 France claims Mississippi and all of the land within the Mississippi River Valley.
EVENT

- 7 -

To keep a large cotton plantation running smoothly, owners needed to have many workers.

State bird: mockingbird

Cotton plantation

French farmers. They planted cotton, tobacco, and rice, and their small farms soon grew into large plantations. Farmers could not do all the work themselves, so they started bringing slaves from Africa in 1719.

France fought England to keep Louisiana in the French and Indian Wars of 1754–1763. The Chickasaw tribes helped the English troops, who took control of Louisiana in 1763. England split Mississippi's land between the colonies of Georgia and South Carolina.

Under English control, colonists were not allowed to make their own laws. They had to pay taxes to England, too. In 1775, the colonies fought for independence from England in the Revolutionary War. The United States won the war and their freedom in 1783.

In 1798, Mississippi became a United States territory. Natchez was named its capital. U.S. president John Adams sent politician Winthrop Sargent to be the territory's first governor. In 1817, the U.S. government divided the Mississippi Territory into two sections. It created the Alabama Territory from the eastern half. The western half kept the name Mississippi and became the country's 20th state. David Holmes, who had been the last territorial governor, then became governor of the state. Settlers moved to Mississippi from

YEAR

1719   The first slaves from Africa are brought to Mississippi plantations.

EVENT

The forests and fields of Mississippi became important battlegrounds during the American Civil War.

eastern states to farm the land. Cotton quickly became the top crop in the state.

Cotton farmers relied on slave labor to keep up with the demand for cotton in the U.S. and Europe. Many people in the North disagreed with the practice of slavery, though. They wanted all slaves to be set free. Since the South opposed this idea, Mississippi withdrew from the Union with 10 other Southern states. These states formed the Confederate States of America and elected Mississippi senator Jefferson Davis as their president. The North did not accept the Confederate States as a separate nation.

The American Civil War began in April 1861. Battles between the North and South went on for four years. In 1862, the Battle of Shiloh was the first to be fought in Mississippi. It was fought to decide who would have control of a railroad in northeastern Mississippi. Confederate troops lost that battle, though, and the Union eventually won the war in 1865.

When Jefferson Davis was three, his family moved to a plantation near Woodville, Mississippi.

YEAR

1729   French settlers force many American Indians out of Mississippi.

EVENT

- *10* -

Majestic Mississippi

FOUR SOUTHERN STATES SURROUND MISSISSIPPI. THE
MISSISSIPPI RIVER FORMS THE ENTIRE WESTERN BOUNDARY
OF THE STATE BETWEEN LOUISIANA AND ARKANSAS.
ALONG THE NORTHERN BORDER IS TENNESSEE. ALABAMA
LIES TO THE EAST. THE GULF OF MEXICO FORMS
MISSISSIPPI'S SOUTHERN BORDER.

The northernmost region in Mississippi is known as the Hills. The Hills extend from the Mississippi River to the state's eastern border. Rolling hills in the west give way to sharp rock ledges in the east near the foothills of the Appalachian Mountains. Bubbling streams cut through forests of hardwoods and loblolly pines, which grow best in low, wet places. Many poultry farms, as well as Holly Springs National Forest, can be found in the Hills Region.

South of the Hills, from the center of the state to the Alabama border, is the Pines Region. Meridian, Columbus, Winona, and Forest are major cities within the region. Waves of hills are forested with loblolly and shortleaf pines. Farmers grow corn and cotton or raise cattle and catfish.

The Tennessee-Tombigbee Waterway system is found in the Pines. The "Tenn-Tom," as it is called, is a 234-mile (377 km) artificial waterway that was completed in 1984. From the Tennessee River at Pickwick Lake on the Tennessee-Mississippi border, it extends south through Mississippi to the Tombigbee River. The Tenn-Tom allows ships from Tennessee and Alabama to get to the Gulf of Mexico by a much shorter route.

Far south of the Hills' Holly Springs National Forest (above) is the city of Natchez, on the Mississippi River (opposite).

YEAR
1763   England wins the French and Indian Wars, claiming Mississippi as its own.
EVENT

- 13 -

T he Coastal Region lies south of the Pines and stretches from the center of the state to the Gulf Coast. Forests cover much of the area. Farmers there grow such crops as pecans and sweet potatoes. Fishermen catch flounder, speckled trout, and shrimp in the Gulf Coast waters. A few miles from Mississippi's coast, five small islands covered with white sand and marshes are preserved as the Gulf Islands National Seashore. Crabs and sea turtles make these islands their home. Bottlenose dolphins play nearby in the shimmering blue waters of the Gulf.

Two of Mississippi's best-known products, shrimp and pecans, are found close to the Gulf Coast, where shrimping boats (above) roam and pecans drop from trees (opposite).

*Soybean harvests are
particularly strong in
five counties within the
Mississippi Delta region.*

Soybean harvest

The Capital/River Region is found in the southwestern corner of Mississippi. This region, home to the state capital, Jackson, is also known as the Black Prairie for its rich, dark soil. Fish abound in the region's many rivers and streams. Fox, swamp rabbits, raccoons, and opossums live among the willow and cottonwood trees. White-tailed deer, wild turkeys, and quail are also abundant. Although farms that produce beef, dairy products, cotton, and catfish can be found throughout the state, they especially thrive in the Capital/River Region. Many natural gas and petroleum mines are also found there.

To the north of the Capital/River Region in the western part of Mississippi lies the Delta. It covers the area between the Yazoo and Mississippi rivers. Lakes and streams in the Delta teem with bass, crappie, bluegill, and catfish. The rich land supports sprawling, corporate-owned farms, which produce cotton, wheat, and soybeans. Farmers in Belzoni County raise more catfish than those in any other county in the U.S.

The climate in Mississippi is mild in the winter and hot in the summer. Temperatures average 40 °F (4.4 °C) in the winter. Summer temperatures often reach 100 °F (38 °C). The light winds blowing off the Gulf Coast do little to relieve the 90 percent humidity that blankets the state during August and September.

Mississippi slash pine trees are cut down and used for their oils or made into paper products.

YEAR
1817 Mississippi becomes the 20th state; Natchez is named its capital.
EVENT

Mississippi Movers

The first people to settle in Mississippi were from France. They built the oldest city in Mississippi in 1699. Today, it is known as Ocean Springs. The French also settled and started farms around Natchez. Europeans from countries such as England, Scotland, Ireland, and Germany were attracted to Mississippi by the rich land of the Delta and Black Prairie.

In the 1700s and 1800s, settlers brought slaves from Africa to work on their plantations. By 1861, there were more African Americans in Mississippi than European Americans. But African Americans did not have the same rights as white people did.

After the Civil War, when all slaves were set free, African Americans were able to pursue their own careers. In 1870, Hiram R. Revels, a pastor from Natchez, became Mississippi's first African American senator. Revels served for one year, and in that time, he worked to create equal opportunities for all people. In 1871, he became the first president of Alcorn State University, a college in the southwestern part of the state.

Today, more than one-third of Mississippi's population is African American, and about 60 percent of people have

In the late 1800s, African Americans could work for pay and get a college education thanks to people such as Hiram Revels (opposite).

YEAR
1861   Mississippi and 10 other states leave the Union to form the Confederate States of America.
EVENT

- 19 -

In the 1950s, two Mississippi-born singers, Muddy Waters (above) and Elvis Presley (opposite), made blues and rock music popular.

European backgrounds. Immigrants from Spanish-speaking countries, China, and Vietnam also live in Mississippi. A large number of Choctaw people still live in Mississippi, too.

Blues singer Muddy Waters was born in Rolling Fork, Mississippi, in 1915. His amplified guitar changed the sound of traditional blues music. It gave blues an edgy, powerful sound in the 1940s and 1950s. He won seven Grammy Awards for his songs, including the 1992 Lifetime Achievement and 1998 Hall of Fame awards.

Rock-and-roll singer Elvis Presley liked the blues and gospel music of African Americans. He was born in Tupelo in 1935 and grew up to become "The King" of early rock music. Presley's birthplace and museum is a popular destination for his countless fans around the world today.

Two modern entertainers also have their roots in Mississippi. Talk-show host Oprah Winfrey was born in Kosciusko,

YEAR

1927 The Mississippi River floods, killing hundreds and forcing the government to reroute the river.

EVENT

- *20* -

while actor James Earl Jones spent the first few years of his life in Arkabutla. Known for his deep voice, Jones has been acting in award-winning movies and plays since the 1960s. Winfrey, who has the highest-rated talk show in television history, was ranked by *Forbes* magazine in 2000 as the richest African American of the 20th century.

Many Mississippians still make a living by farming. It is the state's top industry and brings in $5.8 billion a year. Some grow corn, soybeans, or cotton. Others raise cattle, poultry, or catfish. Since the state's economy depends on agriculture, Mississippi offers unique "agritourism" opportunities for visitors. People can tour cotton farms and discover the history of Mississippi's first king crop, or they can visit catfish museums that tell the story of the fish from "pond to plate." They can even see animals such as buffalo and emu at special parks.

Oprah Winfrey began her storied career in media at age 19 as a news anchor in Tennessee.

YEAR

1939   Oil is discovered near Tinsley, and 133 oil wells are in use by 1941.

EVENT

- 23 -

James Earl Jones

Many Mississippians work in industries that focus on services and manufacturing. Service jobs include those in education, retail, and health. The University of Mississippi Medical Center and Mississippi Baptist Health Systems are two of the state's largest employers. Manufacturing positions can be found in Mississippi's transportation equipment plants. Many well-known companies, including Whirlpool, General Electric, and Chevron, have production plants in Mississippi.

James Earl Jones (above) grew up in the small town of Arkabutla, about an hour's drive northwest of Oxford, home of the University of Mississippi (opposite).

YEAR
1964

Surgeon James D. Hardy, of the University of Mississippi Medical Center, performs the world's first heart transplant.

EVENT

Mississippi Marvels

Each fall, thousands of ruby-throated humming-birds follow a path from Canada, through Mississippi, to Mexico and Central America. The birds fly through the fields and woods of Strawberry Plains Audubon Center in Holly Springs. There, they hover and sip from the Center's flowers and feeders to gain strength for their long journey south.

The Hummingbird Migration Celebration attracts thousands of people to Holly Springs in September. It is one of the largest nature festivals in America. The celebration features live bat and alligator demonstrations, presentations on reptiles, and tours of the historic Strawberry Plains plantation home.

The ruby-throated hummingbird is the only hummingbird found in eastern North America.

Near Natchez, an 8-acre (3.2 ha), flat-topped mound of earth rises 35 feet (11 m) high. Named "Emerald" after a nearby plantation, the mound is one of the largest ceremonial mounds in the U.S. Early Natchez people built the mound, a large trench around it, and eight smaller mounds some time between A.D. 1250 and 1600. The people most likely used the mound for religious purposes or government meetings. A temple and home for the leader or priest was likely built on each end of the mound.

Large plantation homes throughout the South featured tall columns and multiple stories.

Another attraction in Mississippi highlights its more recent past. The Florewood River Plantation State Park near Greenwood allows visitors to see what life was like on an 1850s cotton plantation. The planter's mansion, laundry house, blacksmith shop, sawmill shed, and slave cabins make up some of the many buildings on the property. Park interpreters tell visitors about what people's lives and jobs were like on the plantation.

YEAR

1989 In Fayette, Charles Evers is elected as the state's first African American mayor since the late 1800s.

EVENT

William Faulkner wrote many stories based in a fictional Mississippi county called Yoknapatawpha.

Many homes in Mississippi before the Civil War were lived in by wealthy plantation owners. Homes from this time period are called antebellum, a word that means "before the war." In Natchez, there are about 70 such mansions. Twenty-four of these homes look the same today as they did in the early 1800s. From the fall through the spring, tour guides dress up in costumes from the time period and act like the people who would have lived in those homes.

Mississippi has produced its share of famous people who have left their homes behind as museums. One of the state's most famous writers, William Faulkner, was born in New Albany in 1897. His novels won major awards and are required reading in many classes around the world. People can tour the museum that is now in Faulkner's former house in Oxford.

In Biloxi, on the Gulf Coast, the first cast-iron lighthouse in the South still stands. Built in 1848 by Stephen Pleasonton of the U.S. Treasury Department, the lighthouse towers over Biloxi Bay. It is Mississippi's last remaining lighthouse and was the only one to withstand the winds of Hurricane Katrina in August 2005.

Originally, the Biloxi Lighthouse (pictured) was one of 10 lighthouses along the Mississippi coastline.

2005   Hurricane Katrina devastates Mississippi, affecting nearly 1 million of the state's 2.9 million residents.

QUICK FACTS

Population: 2,910,540

Largest city: Jackson (pop. 179,599)

Capital: Jackson

Entered the union: December 10, 1817

Nickname: Magnolia State

State flower: magnolia

State bird: mockingbird

Size: 48,430 sq mi (125,433 sq km)—32nd-biggest in U.S.

Major industries: farming, petroleum products, electronics

Although Mississippi does not have any professional sports teams, it is the birthplace of many famous athletes. Those Mississippians who have made the record books include football players Jerry Rice and Brett Favre, James "Cool Papa" Bell of baseball's Negro Leagues, and boxer Henry Armstrong.

While Mississippi preserves its historic past, the changing world of high-tech industries is expanding into the state, bringing new opportunities to Mississippi residents. As the state moves into the future, people are working together to keep Mississippi marvelous.

Henry Armstrong boxed professionally from 1932 to 1945, afterwards becoming a Baptist minister.

BIBLIOGRAPHY

Bockenhauer, Mark H., and Stephen F. Cunha. *Our Fifty States.* Washington, D.C.: National Geographic Society, 2004.

Fifty States. "Mississippi: The South's Warmest Welcome." 50states.com. http://www.50states.com/mississi.htm.

George, Charles, and Linda George. *Mississippi.* New York: Children's Press, 1999.

Schubach, Erik. "Mississippi State History." The US50. http://www.theus50.com/mississippi/history.shtml.

SHG Resources. "Mississippi Timeline of State History." State Handbook and Guide. http://www.shgresources.com/ms/timeline/.

Zenfell, Martha. *Insight Guide United States: On the Road.* Long Island City, N.Y.: Langenscheidt Publishing Group, 2001.

INDEX